I0157023

LEAD

Life ~ Emotions ~ Addiction ~ Death

Kim Doran

c2018 Kim Doran. All rights reserved.

No part of this book may be reproduced, stored in a retrieval system, or transmitted by any means without the written permission of the author.

First Published by Kim Doran 12/2019

ISBN #978-1-7369581-0-0

Cover Design by Fabian Allen

Author Photo by Kristen Follano

Printed in the United States of America

LEAD will lead you into a contemplative practice to be with the Lord. Kim's beautifully orchestrated poetry topics will stretch you to pause and feel each word.

The book is needed in our hurry up rushed lives. I encourage you to be still and know God and contemplate where you have been and where you are heading.

Michelle D. Howe
Author of Rise Up and Build Devotional Series
and It Is Finished

Dedicated to:

James Francis McMahon

Dad, you always listened and
told me I could be anything I choose to be.

I miss your heart, your wisdom and your voice.
RIP

Contents

Life:

Emotions:

Addiction:

Death:

Lead . . .

Change

Transformation is key
if you truly believe
old ways can be no more
let trust open the door

No exceptions in rules
no great price or high dues
just change in character
clay to alabaster

Choosing the better way
step forth into a new day
to transform needs action
a true, bold reaction

Deciding today, isn't easy
life keeps us so busy
yet time is rushing by
are you ready to die?

Put the old in the past
today could be your last
transform your heart and mind
open arms you will find

Trust

Don't shun me
cause I chose to leave

Simply accept
and trust I believe

A new plan
was designed for me

Lay down anger
so that you may see

You weren't left
I was simply freed

The door is open
you can follow my lead

Dark

Dark days
showing no sign of light

Fill me
with unnerving delight

Dark ways
are to blame for the pain

I am
now consumed in self vain

Shadows
move in all around me

Haunting
will not let me be

My sin
holding me down so tight

Losing
all sense of what is right

So Filled

So filled with anguish
from the loss
pain seeps through my veins
at such a cost

So filled with turmoil
from the emptiness
the hole carved deeper
with such unfairness

The void has taken control
though I resist
the dark place rules my day
the damage unmissed

So filled with sadness
from the grief
silence sweeps through my mind
leaving behind no relief

So filled with despair
from the passing
numbness takes over
with feeling everlasting

Simple

It is the simple ways
that will best fill the days
no stress over to do
inner calmness renews

Allow the simple in
you will see peace begins
because thinking too much
only fills lives with rush

Time to look all around
no longer sitting bound
now simply make the time
dig beneath all the grime

Simple as simple is
many cannot get this
for too much thought invades
and need gets in the way

Embrace the day with ease
letting go and release
enjoy the simple gift
take time, avoid being swift

Simple living occurs
casting out deters
walking in inner peace
loving life will not cease

Spark

A truth divulged
feelings expressed
an awkward smile
offered in jest

A word so hard
tones so cold
a moment's breath
captured and stole

A lie be told
the pain hits home
falling apart
feeling alone

A decision
tears out my heart
a lonely place
without a spark

Tide

The tide turns and breaks
as the wind blows
memories past me
sea capped white streaks
moving life before me

Yet solitude has a hold
on heart and mind
stopping reasons why
a clouded sky
total mind drift

Everything seems to move
too fast to grip
frantically around me
clear to blurred
covered in sea's mist

Drenched in shame of truth
quick high deludes
hope breaks through
craving to survive
seeking a cleansing re-do

Release

The place I seek
to lay beneath
my head to rest
upon your core
where the sun beams
and warms the earth's floor

This place I find
to come and just be
my mind at ease
nestled in, complete
watching the sway of leaves
feeling life under my feet

This place I need
to release
my body becomes one
with the soil
inner peace fills me
life hanging by a coil

This place I request
at the end
my body to keep
safe and secure
wrapped in His majesty
ready for the one I adore

Mending

The kettle blows hard at full steam
earning her keep, cuts short her dream
drawing her back to mending seams
she is altering for the team

Pouring a cup of tea with cream
taking a few sips, now redeemed
working late with little light beam
her fingers ache, she wants to scream

Very long hours take a toll
her tired hands continue to roll
a deep sigh and wipe of her brow
coming so close she can't quit now

Morning comes, and work is complete
her fingers throb, her body beat
time to rest her head and sleep sweet
tonight, a new deadline to meet

Take Out

Take the me out of it
as I go through this day
wondering why
you put me in this place

Take the me out of it
mountains will stand, rivers flow
each moment
given a chance to show

Take the me out of it
letting the light, you, be exposed
for all
I am to you is known

Take the me out of it
humbly engrossed in this life
to live
before you call me on home

Flowing

Dripping into limbs
traveling slowly
and ooh the sweet heat
I could not resist

Taking me from here
this place of such pain
into some other
I belong again

Floating above ground
moving as I please
no rushing allowed
inhale and release

Tingles through veins
nothing in the way
feeling so supreme
poison is its name

Images in mind
happy at this time
until I do sink
trapped in rewind

Crashing down so fast
as my body shakes
my heavy burden
flowing with mistakes

Vengeance No More

From the Taj Mahal to empire state
wickedness seeps through the earthly gate
a loaded pistol I fire away
taking down all that gets in my way
this was unplanned- blood bath-be it what may
I was longing for a humbled day
but justice rang through my human veins
shooting down the terrible – I gain
now walking alone in this perfect land
valley barren, 'cept a solitary man
I stop in caution and come eye to eye
this is the great reader of my mind
He sees within, uncovers all my lies
love being on top, ego denies
He waits for me to speak and confess
another chance to clear the darkened mess
I stand, back arched, ready to attack
then I see His tear fall, He wants me back
this was not what He planned for my day
total sabotage, life's game gone astray
as I lose my step and my solid stance
knowing this is my very last chance
I lay down my weapon, reach out my hand
seeking forgiveness, as I leave this land

Corruption

Resentment fills my bones
in this I'm not alone
when it can clearly be seen
your side is always green

You take but do not give
is this how we are to live?
Not how I was raised
only God is who I praise

It can't stay this way
we all long for better days
yet you sit so securely
we struggle you see surely

Time to make a change
hope is in full range
staying is no longer an option
can't sit and watch corruption

Stand

I stand before you
a broken woman
a shell of emptiness
with thoughts, out of control

I stand before you
so very torn to the core
a cloud of loneliness
good emotions no more

I stand before you
now bare, with no fight
body without feeling
and eyes defying sight

I stand before you
shattered and hollow
a heart with a huge hole
and no path to follow

Clear Route

A goodbye freed you
from captivity
under the influence
loss of dignity

A time to heal
inside out
under direct care
taking clear route

An inner look
at mind
under no pressure
yet will find

A way to break
addiction's crime
under protection
in due time

A vow to give
up drink
under direct view
your struggles sink

A time to live
without pain
under faith
new life gained

Buried

Why, we will never know
you decided to let go
left us here broken
a note – a life token

Thoughts ran through your head
telling you were better off dead
one less screw up here
life consumed in total fear

Why, will not be answered
speculation from drugs to cancer
yet only you hold the key
as reason consumes me

Hurt buried ever so deep
kept you up, lack of sleep
pain in mind, body and heart
pushed you to fall apart

Why, will forever haunt us
you jumped aboard suicide bus
no justification can be found
simple truth now buried in ground

Bloom

A bouquet in bloom
life for all to see
He's not defeated
lives on in glory

A vast arrangement
all colors galore
His almighty hands
provides the grand tour

A message He sent
for us all to hear
live in harmony
He is always near

A time to reflect
see what He's given
live life faithfully
cherish the living

A world so consumed
with doubt to believe
the beauty abounds
here for you and me

A thank you would please
as He sits and waits
obeying His word
and seeking His grace

Can

Your voice
can soothe me or crush me

Your eyes
can lift me up or harm me

Your touch
can send me or break me

Your words
can fill me or spin me

Your mind
can rule me or destroy me

Your heart
can not belong to me

Wanderer

Wanderer goes around
circles become home
nowhere is where
feet do land up

Lost in the flow
a world so cold
now pushed on past
quickly forgotten

Dismissed as damaged
no hope surfaces
weighed down garbage
smothered in shame

Engulfed in pain
eyes with regret
body depleted
ultimate loneliness

Timed Out

Minute by minute time ticks on
As my heart tells me he is gone
Snatched up from our front yard space
As my mind longs to see his face

Hour by hour passes by
There is no news, I want to cry
Taken from our home and us all
There is no sleep, I wait to fall

Day by day hope slips on its way
As I try to focus and pray
Ripped away from where he belongs
As I struggle to remain strong

Night by night feeling lost inside
What becomes of our hearts denied?
Robbed from all the love we could give
What becomes of the lives we live?

Month by month his face starts to fade
As no new findings have been made
Pulled from our lives with not a trace
As no leads surface with his face

Year by year we still hold out hope
There is nothing left but to cope
Cannot forget our only son
There is only time, what's done is done

Love Not Sword

Let not your guard down
Take a look around
Defeat is running rampant
Too many claiming champion

Armor up to protect
Only take orders direct
Keep focused on what's real
Fall not for any deal

Power is over-rated
Filters hurt and hatred
Instead spread love not sword
Ultimate peace in full reward

Destiny will be claimed
In the house He reigns
As you stand and honor
Thy Holy Father

So That I

The dust swirls
blocking my vision
So that I
cannot see ahead

Leaving me
only with my faith
So that I
walk where meant to be

Excessive Indulgence

Plate filled to the brim
Can't even see the rim
It's piled up high
From floor to sky

An enormous portion
Leading to self-torture
As its stuffed in
How did this begin

No rhyme or reason
An excessive food fest
Indulgence to the extreme
Forfeits reality's dream

Colors and scents galore
Can't witness this anymore
Help is beyond needed
Excessive indulgence is seeded

Leaf

Wind whisks through the trees
Knocking leaves all around
A tender leaf floated down
Upon the ground
Delicately before reaching
Its foreign resting place
Whether it will stay in position
Or move away
All depends on the course
Of action nature will take

Another gust will send the leaf
To land upon some other space
No wind leaves it in place
Circumstance could cause
The leaf to be crushed
And all its memory squashed
Life as a leaf, or human
Has little difference
For where we land
Each end is different

Spared

Tucked and hidden
to avoid the harm
protected in darkness
from wicked charm

Head down low
breath held in close
silence is golden
no time for prose

Still is better
to not be found
movement brings danger
he lurks around

Eyes stare ahead
sweat starts to drip
panic is building
trying to keep grip

Shaking and praying
this will soon end
alarm is ringing
help around the bend

Heart is thumping
cry spills out
sirens are wailing
lights all about

Scared and trembling
from voices calling
shots are fired
bad man falling

Seeing and believing
in answered prayer
lifted into safety
life has been spared

Heard Today

Your voice I heard today
With loving words to say
Good spirits support me
Adding touches of sun rays

Your voice I heard today
Making strides in your way
Concern for my well being
Through the toughest of days

Your voice I heard today
Lift me up from decay
Words and song how I long
In my heart you will stay

Your voice I heard today
Once again, hit re-play
Trusting in survival
My fate is now at bay

Noise

Words of untruth
Spill out
Lies create rumor
Talking about

Feelings get hurt
Judgement comes
Distance is felt
Pain numbs

Center of attention
Not wanted
Fingers are pointed
Now taunted

One who shares
Without truth
Causes utter turmoil
Bad fruit

With selfish ambition
Comes division
Talk is cheap
Unwanted vision

Think before speaking
Gossip destroys
No interest in
Unhealthy noise

In Motion Less

In a town, no name mentioned
On walk the people
Some frown with gloom
Going about what
They need to do
No thinking needed
Programmed to doom
One foot follows, another one ahead
Checking off list
Action in bloom
All are somber
Moving in sequence
Task at hand
Walking without boom
Follow the line, painted in green
Subconscious image
Eyes in zoom
Forward in motion
One step, two
Mindless beings
With little room
No reaction seen, staring ahead
One, two, three
The pace resumes
The heat rises
Crackles and snaps
The fire scorching
Smell the fumes
Empty of feelings, don't care anymore
Onward they walk
As death looms
Tiny steps striding
Merely seeking freedom
Out of this nothingness
Of death's perfume

Connect

Speak from heart
Without malice

To strengthen union
With truth

Promote life honestly
To sustain

Trust without doubt
Of self-gain

Put integrity over
Attention always

Be the hands
That connect

Open and honest
Not dissect

Recognize the beauty
Healthy relationship

Strive to obtain
Not detain

If Ever

If ever you find
Someone so special
Do not deny it

If ever you touch
Someone so precious
Respect you must

If ever you see
Someone so beautiful
Be ever so true

If ever you love
Someone completely
Do tell and trust

Slot

The sound intrigues
With whistles and dings
Lights and colors
All excitement and flutters
So sleek to feel
With buttons and handle
Cherries and sevens
Bring life in numbers
As bells ring
With satisfying delight
Turning of coins
Fills up the night
But what comes
quickly is then gone
as more is spent
leaves you all done
The cycle created
With gadget and tool
To lure you in
Take up the stool
For hours consumed
With hope and greed
Music and drinks
Complete the scene
Chances are slim
In slots and cards
Winners and losers
Will stand apart
The game destroys
With lies and deceit
All sevens rare
Leaving you beat
Quit while ahead
With no need for play
Stand and say
This is not the way
Take no chances
With thrill of game
The lure and bait
Only pulls you down again

Held

It's held me captive
For far too long
Has held me back
From a new song

It's held me prisoner
With locks on the door
Has held me in
A state of war

It's held me victim
Inner scars to show
Has held me close
A hell to know

It's held me ransom
A high price paid
Has held me trapped
As truth now fades

It's held me unforgiven
With doubt and shame
Has held me lost
And living in blame

It's held me broken
And scattered in pieces
Has held me desperate
Ready to release it

New Day

It's a new day for you and me
With your forgiveness
I can put my yesterday away

Together a new path we can take
For you always
Lead the master way

It's a new day for you and me
With your mercy
I can put fear at bay

Together a new road we will follow
For you always
Walk along without delay

It's a new day for you and me
With your grace
I'm transformed without betray

Together we can stay on path
For you always
Shine your light each day

Low

Sounds in my head
Words spill from my lips
The battle is waging
Internal faith slips
Fine wiring short circuits
Lines are being crossed
Truth is dismissing
All hope is tossed
One struggle too many
In this short life
Being faithful is trying
When life cuts like a knife
Clouds before my eyes
As test and trials nerve me
Flooding emotions on alarm
No feeling of being free
Time is lingering
As illness invades
Within this inner shell
All strength fades
Feeling battered down
Energy now lost behind
Physical is a burden
Hopelessness eats my mind
Sinking to my lowest low
Out is the only way
Being scared and alone
Longing to end this day
No one can understand
The pain in my veins
Losing life and losing hope
Angry with He who reigns
Not believing in saving grace
Since living this outcome
Days screaming to be saved
Wanting sickness undone

All About

Always a grand entrance
To make heads turn
Seeking with vengeance
Everyone's attention

It's all I, me and my
Words keep fluttering out
While others just stand by
Trying to figure all about

No room for others
To speak a word
Your tone totally smothers
As we stand unheard

This just can't go on
Domination in full spawn
All patience now gone
Ready to run a marathon

Always a quick retreat
To silence ignorance
Feeling escape under my feet
Tired of irrelevance

But my heart hurts
can't be so cruel
to just up and desert
leaving you all about you

Focus

Penetrate the outer layer
And reveal what's within
Allow the edges to crumble
And the new birth to begin

Hostile behavior is no win
It highlights darkest sin
Instead focus to restore
The you long ignored

Stone Cold City

Curious looks
on faces unknown
Silent tongues
with back view glances
In stone cold city

Putting up
Walls of resistance
Under tones
With icy stares
In stone cold city

A city so cold below zero isn't enough to crack
The hearts and souls of the people
In stone cold city

On lookers
Wanting to know
Cynical minds
With little growth
In stone cold city

Hiding away
Scared to face
Broken spirits
With shattered dreams
In stone cold city

A city so cold below zero isn't enough to crack
The hearts and souls of the people
In stone cold city

Through

When everything around
Spins out of control
Totally fragile and feeling alone
Just know He promised you
He'd see you through and through

When words pierce your heart
And spit you out
Totally naked filled with doubt
Just know He promised you
He'd hold you through and through

When anger is ripe
And leaves you bruised
Totally degraded and unamused
Just know He promised you
He'd free you through and through

When confusion sets in, all consumed
Totally lost and feeling doomed
Just know He promised you
He'd love you through and through

In This Skin

Tight and cramped
In this skin I'm in
Ache and throb
Fingers bent in grip
Whole body reeks pain
From the outside in

Tense and worn
Battling this storm
Stiff and curled
Outer layer to inner core
Whole body deformed
From the inside out

Stress and anger
Yearning for more
Stabbing and fire
Flow through my veins
Whole body reeks pain
From the outside in

Illness and heartache
Rampant within me
Broken and used
All of me, each inch
Whole body drained
From the inside out

Save

With a smile given
Spirits are risen
Kindness isn't dead
Love is daily bread

Reached out a hand
In a harden land
To save a soul
Despair no control

Simply left to die
No one by side
Yet can rise above
In abundant love

Is given without
Price or expectation
Jesus did that
It's called crucifixion!

We Call Life

Steps along the way
Both wrong and right
Create memories
That we call life

Patterns developed
Above all else
Create legacy
That we call life

No one could have known
Can't do alone
Each step He will lay
Another day

Blocks placed in the way
Both high and wide
Create foundation
That we call life

Diversion is found
Consumes all else
Creating the core
That we call life

No one could have known
Can't do alone
Each step He will lay
Another day

Remind Me

Movement in my bones
Remind me
I am not alone

Stirring in my heart
Remind me
I am a part

Longing in my soul
Remind me
A rock to roll

Thoughts in my mind
Remind me
A way to find

Words in my mouth
Remind me
It is all about

Action in my life
Remind me
Do without strife

Let Me

Let me
Let me get my feet
On the ground and watch me run
And watch me run

Stop holding
Stop holding me down
From the road
I'm not meant to be on

All lies
All lies you do tell
Broke my whole
Living in this hell

No trust
No trust not a word
Tore me apart
Cattle in a herd

Denied me
Denied me a true love
Crushed my all
Dreams broken and shoved

Let me
Let me get my hope
Stirred on up and watch me go
and watch me go

Theft

One I could count on
With such a deep bond
Morning noon and night
With you, always right

Time was filled with love
Blessed from Heaven above
To spend our life together
Making us each better

Then chaos tore us apart
Leaving a broken heart
It all happened fast
Forever didn't last

Memories are all that's left
A love story theft
Now once reality
Will come in eternity

Spring Onward

With heads bowed
They moved across the field
Eager to complete the task
For meager wages to yield

Covered in hats and gloves
To protect skin from the sun
The two held baskets full
The reward soon to come

Walking the path of dried green
To the shelter up ahead
Thinking only of the sum gained
Their bones ready for bed

Silence surrounds every step
As the sun beams stronger
Each step heavier in time
Just a little longer

Snap goes the branches
Of trees and grass
Hot beneath their feet
Wanting this time to pass

A sound of breeze
Turns their gaze
Up to the sky above
Two souls squint in haze

The wind shifts
Touching sore necks
Hope for new movement
Hearts no longer wrecked

The sun dims to offer relief
The smell of life sweet
Onward the two walked
Eager to beat defeat

Their stride now lifted
A smile upon their faces
Walking swifter, almost sprinting
Longing to feel this place

Dropping the basket at the door
Collecting their wages
Removing their garments
Fleeing to engage

Toes touch the tender blades
Grass tickles their feet
Slight wind, a gentle kiss
A feeling you cannot beat

The mission left behind
Now surrounded in delight
No more heavy loads
Shredded the dread and fright

Manifest

There is nothing you can do
That would close the door
On the love He has for you

No judgement cast upon you
As you search for answers
On how to get through

Life often makes us frail
With hurt and hardness
Stirring up the wanting to bail

Yet remaining ever so still
Allowing Him to guide you
According to His mighty will

Can open the door to trust renewed
A willing heart broken and bruised
An up close and personal view

Surrendered- the battle diffused
As you move beyond the past
Shame and blame no longer glued

Focusing on the love He shows
As His mercy and grace shapes and molds
Creating faith that surfaces and grows

His design manifest as you
Step into the purpose He formed
Revealing a love like you never knew

Pull

Come and lift me
From inner shame
Pull me up pull me out
Of life's turmoil

Come and lift me
Away from the pain
Pull me up pull me out
Of certain dismay

Come and lift me up
From dark ways
Pull me up pull me out
Of selfish gain

Come and lift me
Away from self
Pull me up pull me out
Of troubled days

?

Is there a heart
Within you beating
And a soul tucked down below

Are there two eyes
Open for seeing
And two ears
Tuned for hearing

As this chaotic
And crowded world
Self-destructs
Quickly losing what's known

Raw

Coolness in my palms
Filtering soil with strong arms
Lots to do in this place
Creating a new living space

Digging down hands buried deep
The core of the earth consumes me
Hands tug at the packed soil
Grabbing at life's coil

Grinding in with bare fingers
The moistness wants to linger
Plunging further with all my might
The earth resists and holds tight

Reaching down on bent knees
The dirty hole engulfs me
Covered in muck and soot
All my energy this task took

Set to conquer but not destroy
Wanting a garden to enjoy
Climbing out I ask the Lord
To release all that is stored

Like the parting of the water
He delivered, no longer solid mortar
Free at last to believe
Tenderly I plant the seeds

Seen

Have seen it
In young and old

Seen in myself
If truth be told

Where things said
Show bleeding heart

And it all starts
Slowly falling apart

Facing The Furnace

Another street corner
Booming with business
It's always rush hour
All victims, no witness

The lights dim
As product is given
Looking out over rim
Of buyers, all driven

Lives are diminished
As greed controls
Hopes and dreams are finished
As addiction unfolds

On our streets
Sellers and buyers order
Where destruction meets
Crossing all borders

Facing the furnace
All up in smoke
Craving and yearning
Claiming all folks

Time is running out
The heat is burning
Drugs on all routes
As soil is turning

Anew

Dig a little deeper
And embrace what awaits
Be that creative dreamer
Step out in faith

Take that first step
And up your pace
Be that believer in depth
Show a true face

Walk in good health
Awaken inner spirit
Motivation is your wealth
Do not fear it

See with eyes anew
Forward you must strive
Lead in all you do
Hindered not – become alive

Reflection

Do you fear that image you see?
Because it tells of all you be

Stepping in front of the glass pane
Closes the door of worldly fame

Locking eyes with your self-image
Well now does your smile diminish?

Reflection of the outer shell
Can trick us into all is well

But when you reach to look real deep
Your heart will speed, your feet will leap

Getting past the exterior
Now reveals the interior

No longer concerned with the view
Knowing the deepness within you

Seeing clearly has benefits
Gone are the days of regrets

The vision lifts your heart and mind
True reflection, a humbling find

In

In a fury
Words and threats fly

In the storm
Love crumbles and dies

In the battle
Walls mount up

In the moment
All reaction defies

In the need
Right is wrong

In the silence
No one wins

It Was

Morning comes with renewed hope
Seconds to moments on life's dope
Not needing any alteration
Living full of admiration

The process of self- transformation
No longer dealing in negotiation
Remembering how it once was
And the negatives it does

Staying focused on the now
Living clean, living the wow
Trusting it's all behind
Victory a beautiful find

Heart and mind filled with joy
No longer a broken toy
Too many times on the ground
Overwhelmed by the turn around

Mind's Eye

In my mind's eye
I see a darker side
That creeps on up
And consumes inside
Leaving me guessing
Whether I want
To live or die

Memories flood my mind
With all attempts denied
Shifting with fright
Causing me to wake
Leaving me confused
Whether I am
Too far gone

The Way

Do not be frightened
For He will show you the way
Your world just brightened
As He walks you through your day

For if you can trust
He will show you what is true
All faith is a must
It's time- salvation is due

Many try to advance
But many, becomes a few
From the first glance
He delivers upon you

Now come do your part
Step on out and bring your kin
Open up your broken hearts
Lift up your hands, let Him in

Do not be weary
For He guides by direction
Your path seen clearly
He fills you with affection

For if you believe
He will protect you each day
No need to deceive
He promises you the way

Time

Time can be so cruel
Or it can be a blessing
When faced with the unexpected
One does not know
Which way is best
Until in the shoes, unprotected

Time can be wasted
Or it can be wanted
When living with disease
One does not feel
Beyond the physical pain
Until in the heart, a reprise

Time can be a curse
Or it can be a precious gift
When given a second chance
One does not believe
The suffering will end
Until the mind, can freely dance

Lost Control

Eyes went blurry
A thick haze
Cast over my sight
Presenting a blinded maze

Panic stirred within me
A lost control
My head feeling dizzy
All senses now unknown

Body tingles wildly
A burning declared
Captured all my limbs
Filling me with fear

Trepidation in bones
A lost control
Now movement breaks down
And invades, swallowed whole

Heart races rapidly
A ferocious tone
Pumps through my earlobes
A beat ready to explode

Vision slowly regained
A warped phase
In a survival mode
No way to explain

Coming Around

Numbness in bones
Staring straight ahead
Throat making groans
Not hearing what's said

Just lying there
Heart slowly beating
Total calm, no fear
Ready for the meeting

Movement no more
Body shutting down
Heaven's open door
Is coming around

Peace comes about
As physical decreases
Light illuminates doubt
As soul releases

Be Led To Lead

Feel His presence
Reach out to His hand
For He will guide you
Where no one else can

Let Him take lead
Step beyond in trust
Seek out His counsel
Brush off the old dust

Know that He is near
His spirit flows free
Just wait to hear
It will come to be

Darkness no more
Now the light will shine
Within your lost soul
Your purpose defined

His word is clear
Turn to, not away
Step into His arms
With his hands to clay

He will mold you
And use you to lead
Test will come and go
As you become complete

Conceive

Truth be told
the news filled
with alarm

Timing is wrong
life now altered

Moments of flesh
good, now gone
and beyond

Left to decide
not feeling right

Filled with fear
nowhere to turn
all alone

Afraid to tell
life out of control

Want to run
just pack up and go
far from

So, no one knows
what's been done

So emotional
needing some help
here and now

Movement within
growth begins

Heed

It's a dangerous game
Underground is insane
Dark and seedy places
Sin filling up spaces

The lure to draw you in
The sounds and sights spin
A web of brutal lies
This lifestyle defies

Pulled into the deceit
Your heart frantically beats
Seeing all the gain
Spurred up, created in vain

Faces all are distorted
As pills are assorted
Passed around in pleasure
Becoming tarnished treasure

Time is of the essence
Heed now in your presence
Run for your very life
Before cut by the knife

Escape anyway you can
Run far from evil man
Heed with all you are
Flee now, avoid the scars

The Judging Eye

When time unfolds
Right before your eyes
And chills run
Up and down your spine
You'll know
That it is time
To live in fear
Of the judging eye

When everything
Around you strays
And hope fades
Far and wide left behind
You'll know
That it is time
To live in fear
Of the judging eye

Life Is

Life is
what we live
While here
we take, we give
And sometimes
our path is short
Now over
Like an ending report
But the
glory is in knowing
We will
One day be showing
And Heaven
will be the treasure
To see
again, those we cherish
Be in
that very place
And there
will be your space
Trust in
our God of truth
And you
While here are living fruit

There

You came early
In the mornin'
A beautiful
Sight to see

So small in size
Yet quite mighty
Wings outstretched
Colors depth delight

Your presence
Brought me such peace
The messenger sent
To remind me

Your amazing stare
Focused in on me
No words needed
Showed love abound

Open all eyes
To beauty galore
Everywhere we are
You are always there

In The Midst

Only excuses found
As misery burst
Stuck in the midst
With a sinister twist

All signs present
A battered peasant
Falling in defeat
Of enemy's retreat

Nothing goes right
A losing fight
The battle surrendered
In devious splendor

No rhyme or reason
For this lifeless season
Been taken hostage
And life altered

Desire to be freed
Has not been seen
Comfortably standing by
With echoing cries

Fallen into the pit
Day in you sit
Not reaching the hand
Or rising at command

Pass

Closed eyes
For the last time

As we
Know here on earth

Sorrow comes
As we feel alone

Pain deep
Through heart and bone

Yet life
Has now begun

With Him
Now pass and live

Closet Door

What's behind is barely seen
All the pieces of the screwed up me

Tucked safely in scattered debris
Years long gone tugging to be free

Closed tight no air to breathe
Secrets and lies still within me

Slowly dying a diminishing light
My spirit fading freedom losing sight

What's behind the closet door
Is hindered life wanting no more

Pushing out to break hold
Confess is mounting against the mold

Held firmly in utter seclusion
Mind is racing and rejecting solution

Total darkness not just quite
For a shimmer peeks in light

What's behind seeks a way out
All the broken pieces to shatter about

Finally, ready to reveal self
Confessing wrongs seeking help

The Right Side

On the right side
He is seated
He knows your destiny
The giver of life
Is all you ever need

He walks along
On the right side
He knows your thoughts
The forgiver of sin
Is all you ever need

He stands by
He waits on you
On the right side
The merciful Lord
Is all you ever need

He can catch you
As you fall
He will answer all
On the right side
Is all you ever need

Life just isn't without Him
Once you commit
You will know
He's all you'll need
On the right side

Restless Wonder

My thoughts are so lost
Confusion has me out of sorts
Wanting what cannot be
Is making a mess out of me

Nights are filled
With restless wonder
No answer in sight
To lift me from under

These past months
Have made a mess out of me
Filling me with doubt
And creating endless need

Nights are filled
With restless wonder
No answer in sight
To lift me out from under

So much longing
Has turned into pain
Not knowing what to be
Needing to feel whole again

Nights are filled
With restless wonder
No answer in sight
To lift me out from under

Sheer Love

Just no one like you
Loyal by my side
Every morning and night
Until the day you died

Missing your sweet face
So close to mine
The walks day and night
Now lost in time

No other can replace
The sheer love you gave
The great protector
Always so brave

This place feels strange
Without you here
Human's best friend
Your spirit is near

Home ?

Is this what we call home?

Graffiti all over the place
Madness rules the human race

Beggars in the subway cars
Perverts in the city bars

Sellers on every street corner
Buyers, our sons and daughters

Drugs and murder rule the streets
Cops killed walking their beats

Tell me now, is this what we call home?

Hate all over the place
Greed consumes the human race

Junkies driving subway cars
Disease spreads in city bars

Homeless on every street corner
Losers, our sons and daughters

Hate and fear rule these streets
Kids killed playin' with defeat

Tell me why, this is what we call home?

Fragility

In the tender moments
Exposure of fragility
Peeks out from within
Showing fear and courage

Allowing the opportunity
Beneath made visible
The longing to give
Glory to Him so near

Ready and able to rescue
Exposure of fragility
Swept up and away
From the danger of self

Sunken

The blank look
The stare ahead
A page in a book
Words are dead

The pain's real
The choice hard
A body to steal
Mind on guard

The reason why
The reality showing
A love gone dry
Hurt all knowing

The fact's clear
The heart sunken
A sign of fear
Spirit is drunken

The hope gone
The dream denied
A song done
Addiction is supplied

The truth lost
The pain revealed
A life tossed
Used, trust failed

Mugged

The night was cold
And ever so dark
As I walked
Dogs started to bark
Came on me so fast
And fear rose within
My small frame
Jumped out of skin

Two faces wanting me
To give up and in
But inside I screamed
They will not win
A fight it became
Tooth and nail brawl
Yelling and pushing around
But I would not fall

Off one ran
My stuff in his hands
Leaving another standby
With different plans
Our eyes now locked
Each defending our position
It swelled up inside
As I aborted his mission

Shoved so very hard
Sent him railing down
Losing his balance
And hitting the ground
Shock all over his face
Witnessing my inner strength
Now who was victim
A warrior at arm's length

He rose up from the pit
And quickly backed away
Eyes blaring with fright
For what he saw that day
Tables turned as he ran
Me chasing after him
Full emotion took control
As anger left all my limbs

Retribution

Been accused of a crime
I did not commit
Know none of the facts
Just fit the descript

Tons of pressure
To catch the suspect
Clues none, yet
I'm their prospect

Won't go down in shame
Shackled in a room
Where all judge me
Set my life for doom

Silence they tell me
Is my only defense
But need to scream
Out my innocence

I cry retribution
Must clear my name
Seeking justice
In this crooked game

Start a revolution
Won't take the blame
Screaming retribution
Against this false claim

A...

A tinge of pain
Can be replaced
With hope and prayer
Revival is near

A moment to think
Can be the link
Between joy and despair
Showing we care

A heart that feels
All that is real
Will beat a new tune
Pulled from ruin

A mind that's clear
Will surely hear
A new way to be
Is now set free

Cut

The book brings life
To the lost now found
Gone is the knife
You long carried around

Plunge deep in the words
Soak in the safety
Instead of carving birds
In flesh so blatantly

Take time to listen
To love freely given
See what was missing
while you were digging

Seep into raw skin
And learn this tool
Not like you have been
Slicing, the enemy's mule

Give up this habit
Now is the time
No more draining rabbit
It's a bloody crime

You're not meant to harm
Self or any other
Don't remain the pawn
Be freed my brother

Died Of Self

Like Saul on the road
to Damascus
From rage and murder
To warrior
His sight was taken
Then restored

As was his heart
To heart
From lost and absorbed
To found
His life got shifted
Turned around

Now walking on as Paul
To share
From far and near
To love
his struggles became great
in despair

But on he traveled
To tell
From one to many
To live
His life died of self
With mercy

Unto

The wounds of life cut ever so gently
Not
As each intense moment ticks on
Crush
What hope within offers new beginning
Take
As selfish ambition matter over life
Reflect
Face only image heart so torn
Bleed
A life-line loss of meaning
End
Of a union out of greed

Do unto me as I do unto you

Breathe
In deep, freely love unselfish
See
Offer heart sweetly inspire the needy
Touch
Faces of diversity yearning to be
Taste
Perfume of humanity scenting beautifully
Hear
The bells ringing heart pulses beating
Love
Without a ransom in any condition

Do unto me as I do unto you

Range

Walk with good intentions
Yet often filled with tension
So easy to get rattled
Feeling locked in shackles

Time eats my mind
Raging battle it finds
Doing best I can
Still feeling less than

Others come and go
Treating life like a show
No loyal commitment
Living ever so flippant

Anger boils up inside
All positive now defied
Why do I care so much?
Am I out of touch?

Something must change
Hope is still in range
Maybe it's time to let go
Find another path to sow

Heart is what I am
I truly give a dam
So, I will continue
To look through another window

Engrossed

Bundle of shame
As you sit
Covering your face
Huddled in the screen
Images before you
As you look
Wanting some more
Losing all control
Locked in place
As eyes widen
And mind flows
So insanely engrossed
All darkness unfolds
As you indulge
The sickness grows
Way out of control
Regret soon comes
As you know
This is so wrong
Hurting everyone
Now crying out
As you break
Sin consumed soul
Burning all control
There is hope
As you face
What you do
Wanting no more
Confession is must
As you seek
Redemption to trust
Break through control
Close down screen
As you believe
You are healed
From evil's lust
Turn now instead
As you renew
To the pages
Of life given you

Mangled Tranquility

I am no great mystery
I am exactly what you see
Like a ship sunken near shore
As the waves of life crash no more

Gone is the rhythm under my feet
And no sound of heartbeat
Pushed and shoved once too much
Last straw opened dark door

Wanting to let go be gone
For misery went on and on
Slipping out of reality
Tragedy has mangled tranquility

Laying still beneath sheets
No movement or sound stirs thee
Machines hum and lights blink
While life lingers on the brink

Blessings

May every day
Grant you blessings everywhere you stay

May you feel God's heavenly hands
Follow you throughout the lands

May you know peace and love
As sent from the Lord above

May your heart be filled with grace
And let Him consume your every space

May your days never be dull
For with Him you are full

May you rest safe and assured
That He follows you abroad

May your home glisten with light
And your journey be blessed with God's delight

Adored

Belly full to the rim
As life beats within
Moving left to right
A blessed sight

Cravings all the time
Fingers dipped in slime
Loving all the taste
Nothing goes to waste

Time to feel great
Not worried about weight
Little one growing strong
Got me singing songs

Feeling all uplifted
And thankfully gifted
I'm humbly awaiting
All fear deflating

Soon we will see
Precious one within me
Answered prayer for sure
The one I adore

One much longed for
Impossible no more
Ready to be bore
And forever adored

Ever Growing

In the midst of obstacles
You are holding on to me
Through all my struggles
Right where you said you'd be

While I'm under prosecution
There is no justice to see
Limbs bound up in chains
Yet you come to rescue me

Let me have unwavering faith
Keep me grounded in your name
Ever growing, stirring in me
Until I am totally free

Under attack with no covering
You come and shield me
Through all my battles
Right where you said you'd be

Facing all the demons
Surfacing out from me
Kept captive in bondage
Yet you come to rescue me

Let me have unwavering faith
Keep me grounded in your name
Ever growing, stirring in me
Until I am totally free

Sweet Bird Fallen Flight

The sight of you
Flying in the sky
In great synchronicity
Fills me with awe
And wonder as to
How big it all is

Fluid motion unveiled
Freedom in flight
In great rhythm
Soaring day and night
And life as to
How precious it all is

Yet life unpredictable
Each moment not known
In great longing
Always striving for more
And answers as to
How abundant it all is

Free flowing now falling
From sky to ground
In great sorrow
Fills me with pain
And death as to
How quickly it all is

Lost

Which way to go
Direction unknown

Stuck in place
Desperation shown

Roads all scrambled
Feeling alone

Signs of confusion
Anxiety prone

Path is unclear
Uncertain roam

Highway lingers on
Seeking home

Today

Today
I sit and stare out
At all around me

Not knowing
If I belong
Where my feet are planted

Today
I think and pray out
For all those around me

Not knowing
How not to hurt
If my feet change their path

Today
I feel so far and lost
With all round me

Not knowing
If the path ahead
Will take me to the path back

Toxic Chaos

You made a promise
You did not keep
Each day twisted
Started clean sweep
On and on you dreamed
Bigger than life's reality
All energy was spent
Raw emotional insanity

You tried to quit
But habit was thick
Nipping at your mind
All anxious and sick
Today in and tomorrow out
You chased the rattle
Yet always fell down
Following the sound of battle

Days in total blur
No focus just haze
Life moved on around you
Caught in a deadly maze
Nights in toxic chaos
Beaten down in despair
Low was not low enough
Lifeless without a care

Wide eyed staring ahead
Marks on every inch
Skin so swelled up
No room left to pinch
Death is knocking hard
Existing in rotten core
Waiting for the final high
As eternity opens the door

Some

When the sound of laugher
Hurts your ears
And music plays
But you can't catch the beat
Some just don't understand

When the sun comes up
You are down
And rain drops fall
But you can't feel the pour
Some just don't understand

When time stands still
You can't move
And days go
But you can't see the flow
Some just don't understand

When loss consumes you
Nothing else matters
And time stops
But you can't let go
Some just don't understand

Year's End

Here it is again
Another year has reached its end
All the good and bad
Is now a distant memory

Visions of the days
Learning this created place
All the hope and strength
Is carried humbly within me

Tomorrow brings truth
Time to reflect and be grateful
All the love and health
Are blessings not expectation

A new year begins
Setting goals eager to believe
All the time and hurt
Is past and a new way begins

Dismissed

What you thought
Could not happen
Did
You messed around
And yes produced
Kid
All was great
Until your reality
Hit
All things changed
You threw a
Fit
Being a mom
So not wanting
This
Out you go
Your infant
Dismissed
That little face
You now left
Behind
Laying in crib
Without parenting
Undefined
Crawl back in
Now stinking of
Gin
You messed up
Bottom of the
Bin
A night out
With no harm
Done
As baby lays
Neglected, substituted for
Fun

Stuff

It comes at a price
High bills look so nice
Crisp to the touch
Gives such a rush

Money is what it's about
Old faces looking out
With names most can't spell
Filling up wishing wells

But it don't buy peace
A quick fix of release
From the daily grind
Giving a superior mind

Mounting up material
Feeling so surreal
As the objects exist
Because just can't resist

Does it fill a need?
Or addiction of greed
More is not better
Want and debt together

But it don't buy health
A fake look at wealth
From mere compulsion
To financial destruction

Rage

Told I couldn't
Even when I tried
Told I wouldn't
Even when I cried
You held me closer
Than I wanted to be
You held me down
When I wanted to be free

Every minute of the day
Your words so cruel
Every hour of night
Under watch by you
Living this is insane
Your never-ending rage
Scares me to death
Tears on every page

Not part of the plan
Time filled with pain
And constant injury
Vows down the drain
A total change
In who you are
Got me running
So extremely far

From kisses to punches
Can't do it anymore
Heart is so broken
Behind a glass door
Mister good gone bad
Washed love like rain
I tried to cover
Up all the pain

Each time gets worse
Aching body and mind
This is not normal
No reason to find
It's time to go
Get up and flee
All this insanity
I now clearly see

Thank You, Lord

Thank You Lord
For the sun
That brightens each day

Thank You Lord
For the love
You have sent my way

Thank You Lord
For my life
Which I've taken for granted

Thank You Lord
For my sight
Of how precious life is

Thank You Lord
Yes, Thank You Lord
For always blessing me

Saw

I felt the distance
I saw the eye movement
The surroundings were cold
The bitterness quite bold

I felt the mockery
I saw the tighten lips
The environment was transparent
The un-wanting quite apparent

I felt the disconnection
I saw the heads turn away
The situation was disbelieving
The drama quite deceiving

I felt the laughter
I saw the faces grinning
The room was no longer welcoming
The true colors unsettling

Arise

Face of shame
Is your name
Walking in disgrace
Losing the race
Guilt all over
Sinking you lower
Cry out in pain
Feeling so insane

Choices were poor
Laying on floor
Beating one up
Shaking empty cup
Enemy is self
Dreams on a shelf
Mind comes around
No good sound

Purpose been defied
Filtered with lies
Deception is blind
On hell's ride
Got to find
Strength of mind
To push through
And release you

Let hope arise
And freely cries
To be restored
Reborn and adored
Do not quit
Just simply sit
Let the power
Be watch tower

Count on Him
Light never dim
Be renewed
Lose the feud
The fight ends
When heart mends
Claiming all joy
No longer hell's toy

On This Day

Lay you down
For all to see

Sweetly loved
Forever will be

Now letting go
Left with memories

All my heart
Filled with stories

On this day
Love and pain

In the ground
Come now rain

Now at peace
Head to feet

An eternal life
Maker to meet

All these poems reflect life as we all journey through it differently. My hope is that you found these words a reflection of your journey or that of a loved one. When we show compassion for what someone has walked through and share our ups and downs growth and healing comes for all involved.

May you be blessed and know our struggles make us into overcomers. As overcomers we can offer hope to anyone that feels hopeless. This journey is not meant to walk alone, reach out a hand and walk someone through the valley…better days are ahead for it is promised.

"for such a time as this." Esther 4:14 NIV

Thank you, Paul and Kira, you two have blessed my life beyond measure.
Thank You mom, Susan, for saying "Yes you can!"
Thank you to my friends that encouraged me to write this book and for your honest reviews of my poems.
Thank You God for the gifting, without You there would be no words.

About the Author...

Kim Doran resides in Jensen Beach, Florida with her husband, daughter and mother. She made a career as a Private Investigator until a cancer battle forced her to retire in 2010.

She has overcome cancer and has been actively involved in ministry over the past eight years; and is the founder of *Ladies of Legacy* and founder of *LIFT (Ladies Inspiring Faith and Truth)*.

Kim serves on her church worship team, is Co-editor of her church newsletter and engages in speaking venues to encourage and inspire women. She also enjoys writing, photography, live music, exercise and being out in nature.

Kim is currently working on her next book. She has vowed to finish the works she has piled up on the back burner for not a single day is guaranteed.

www.ingramcontent.com/pod-product-compliance
Lightning Source LLC
Chambersburg PA
CBHW032010040426
42448CB00006B/567